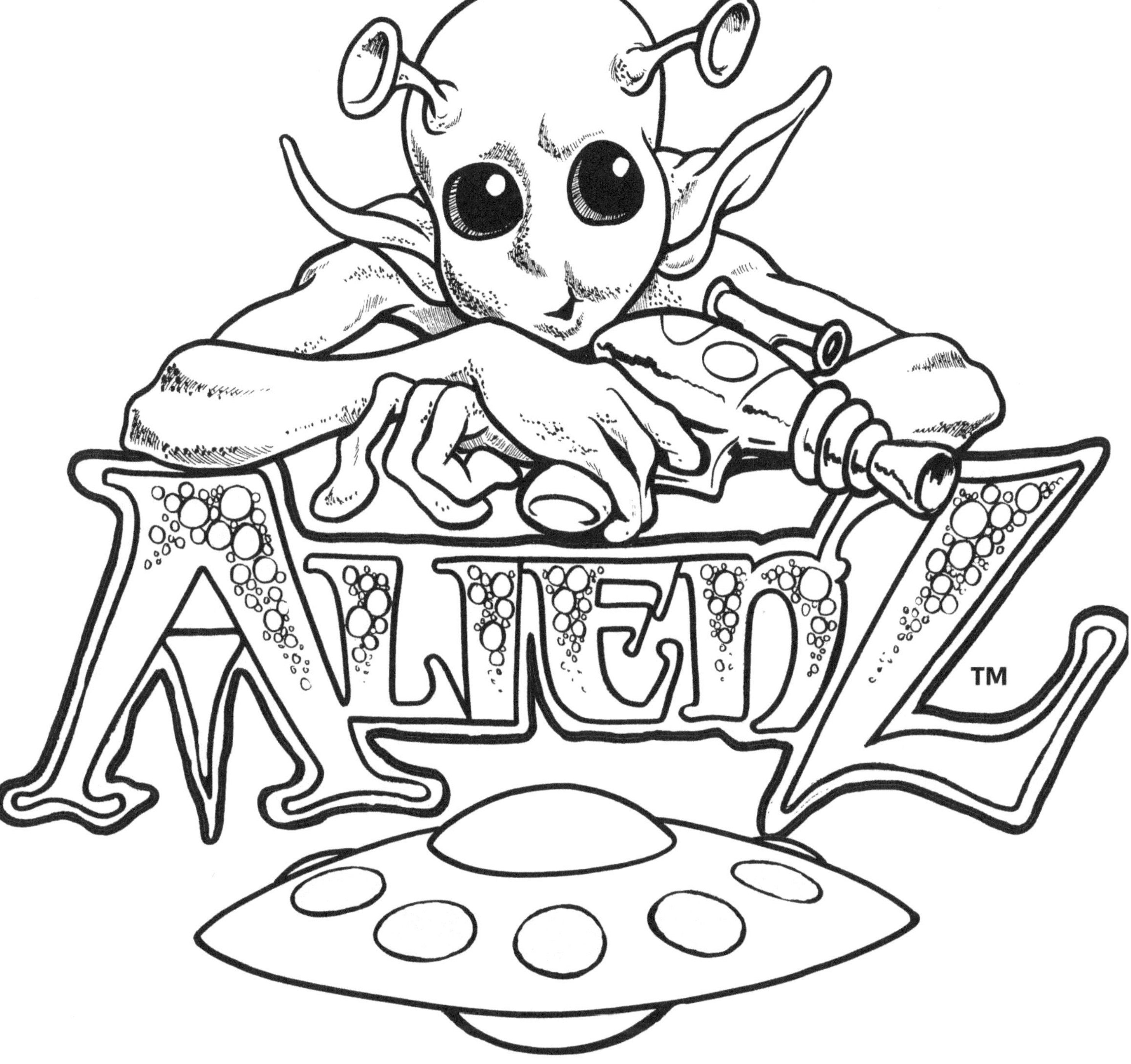

Made in U.S.A.

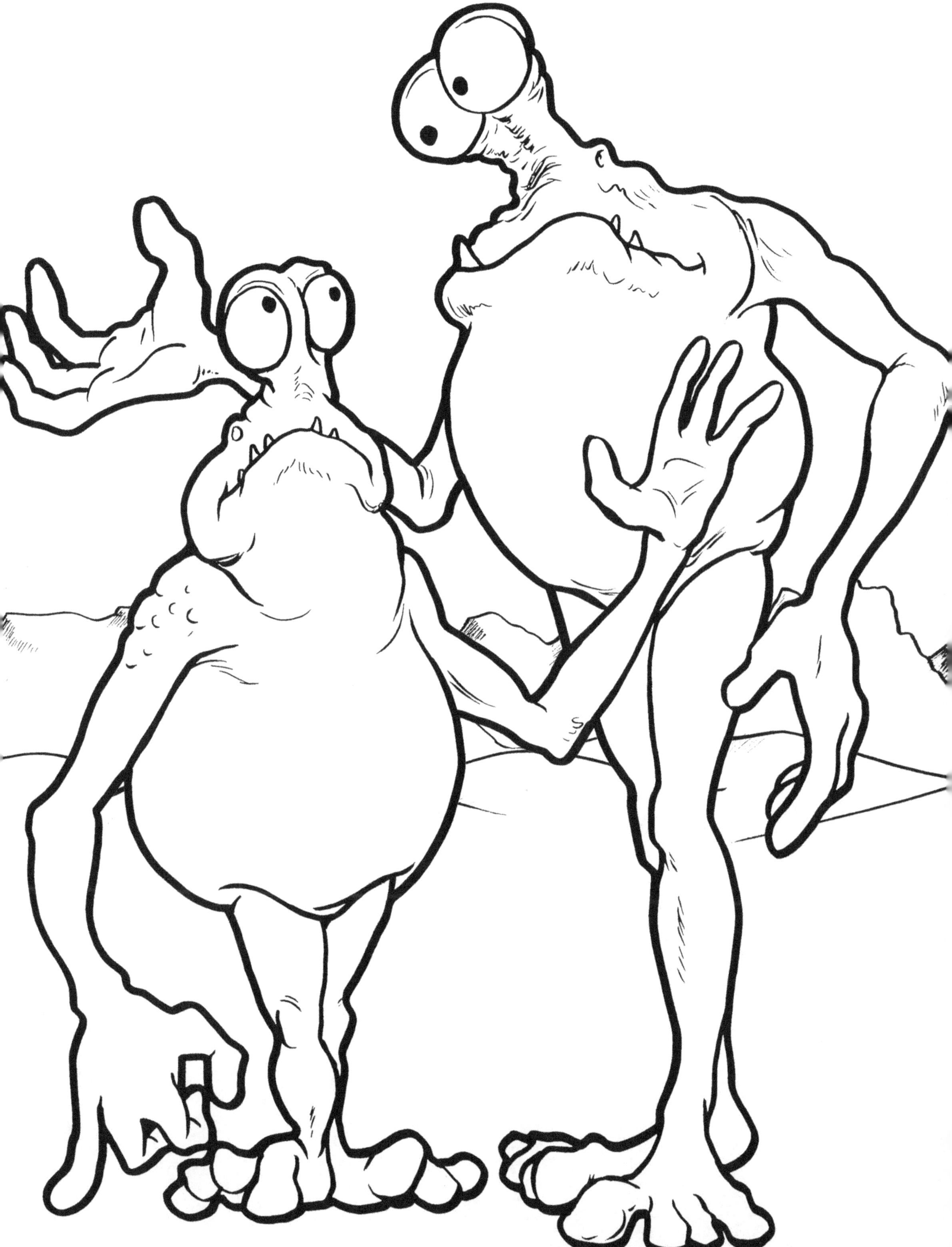

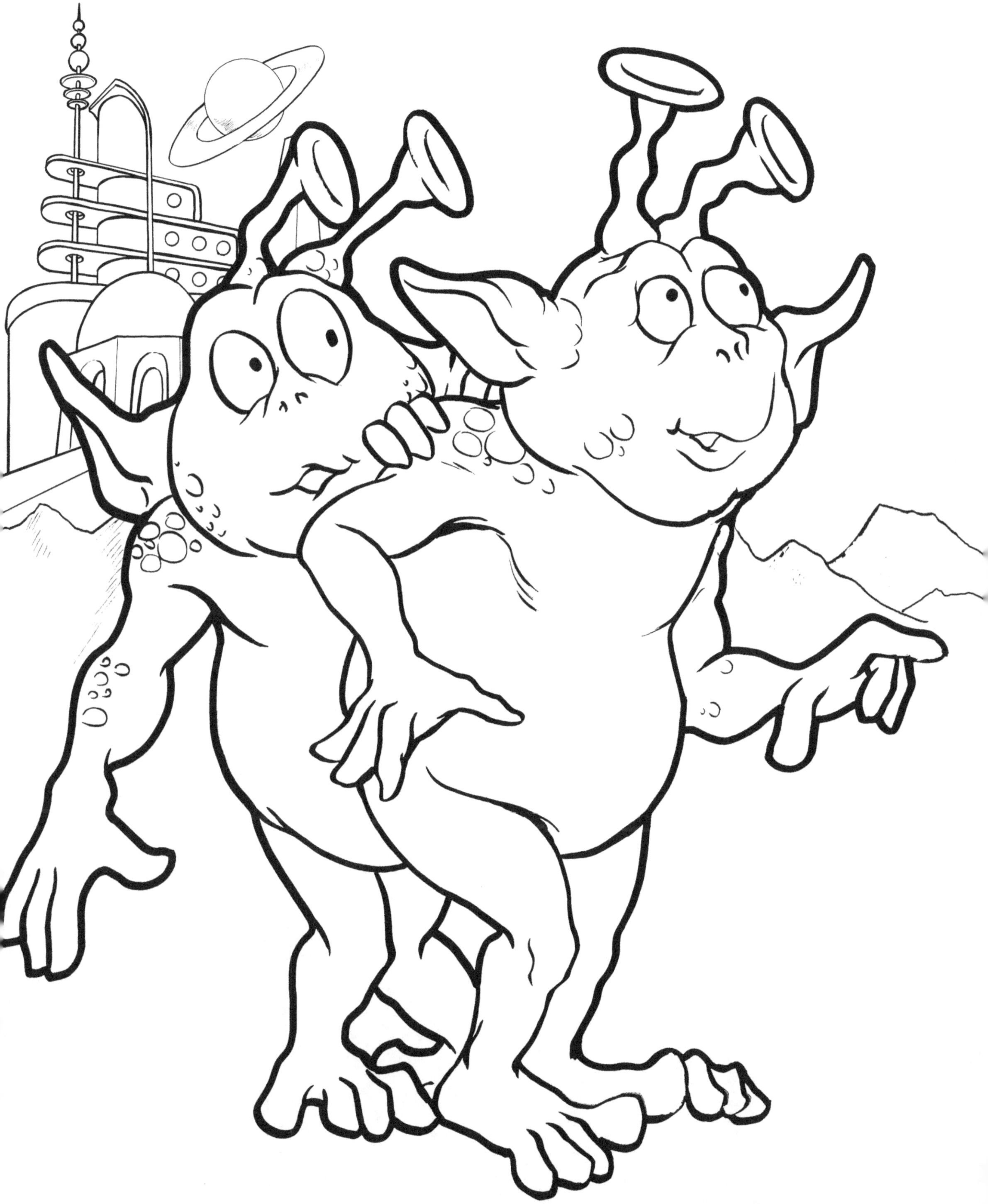

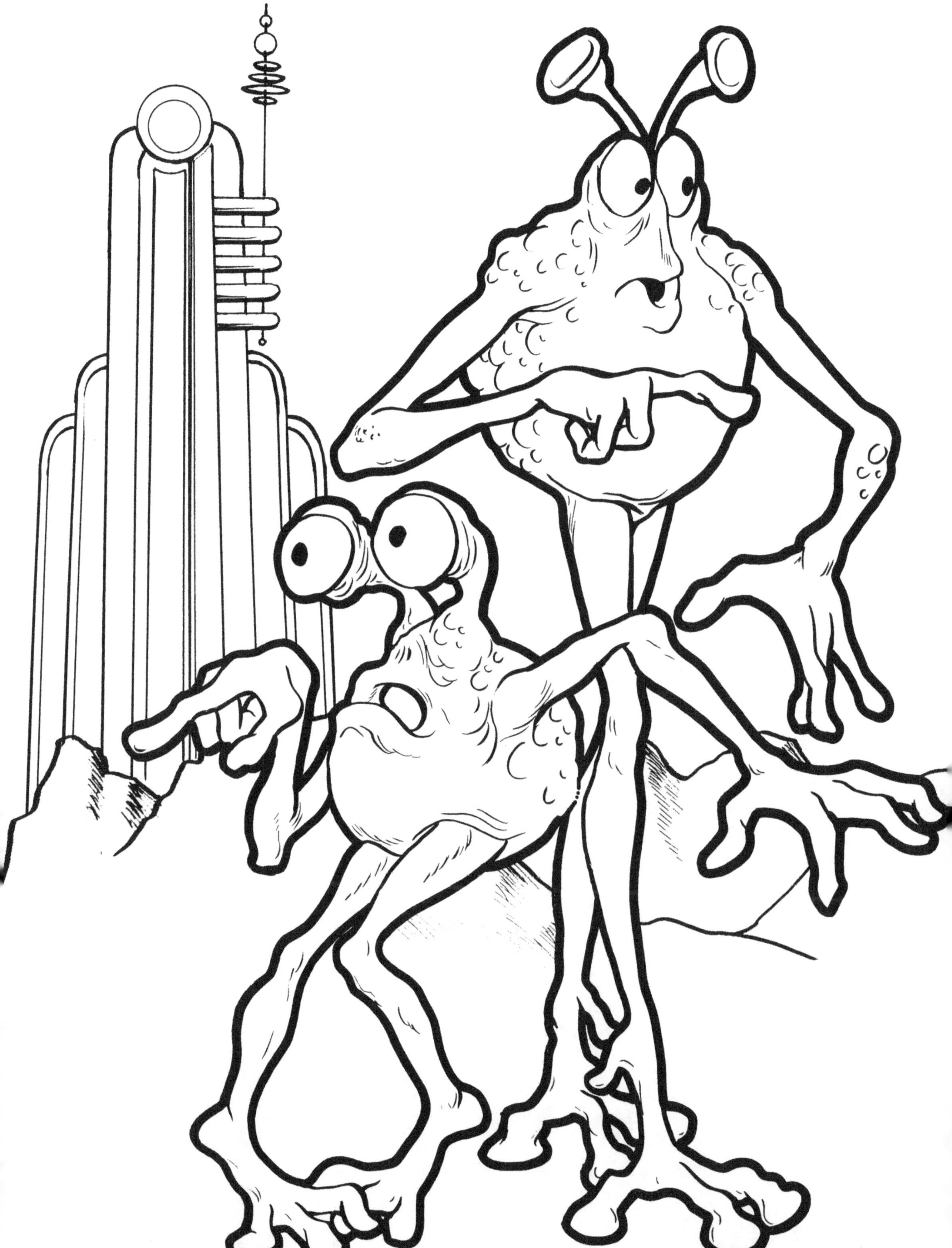

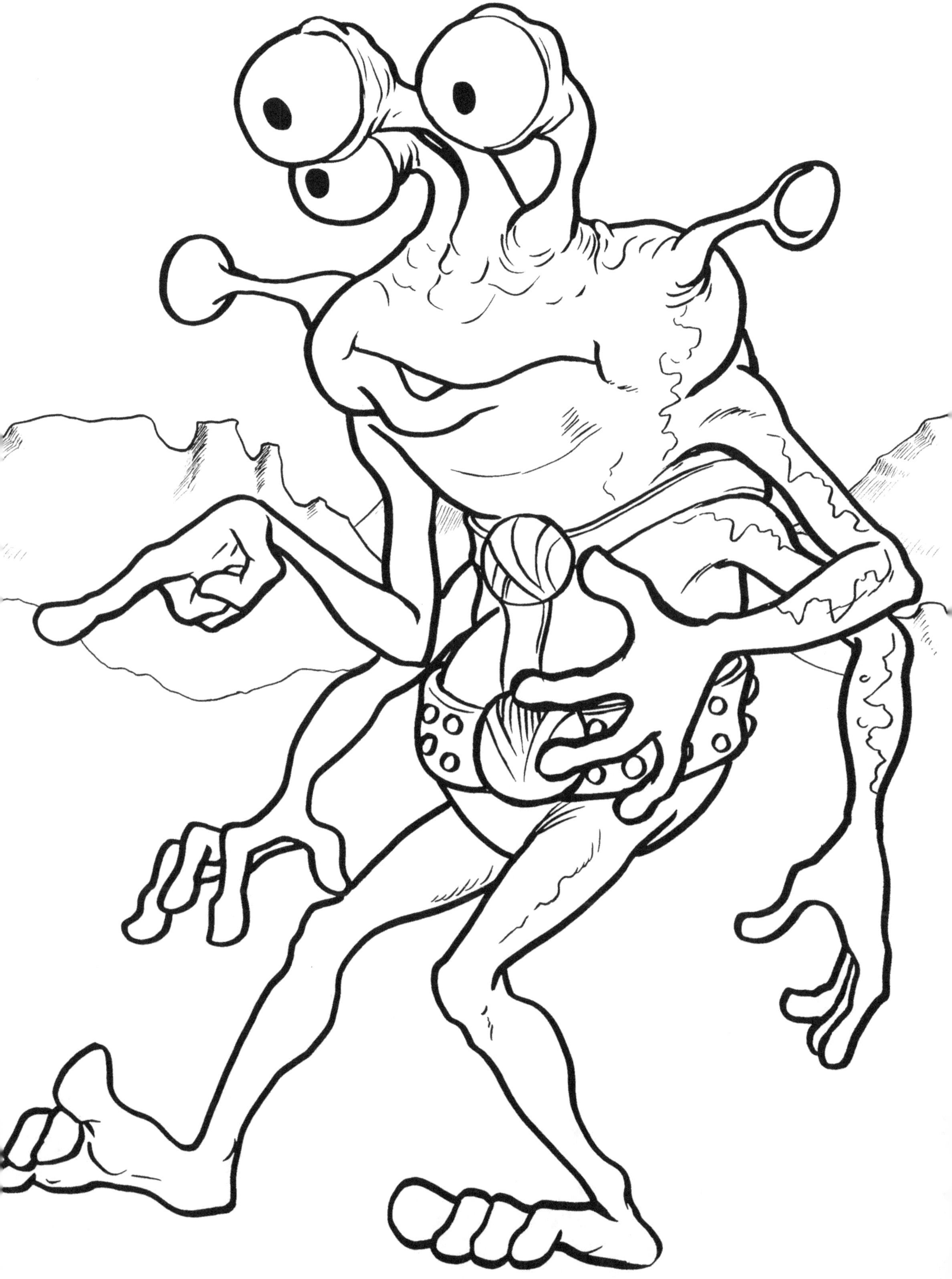

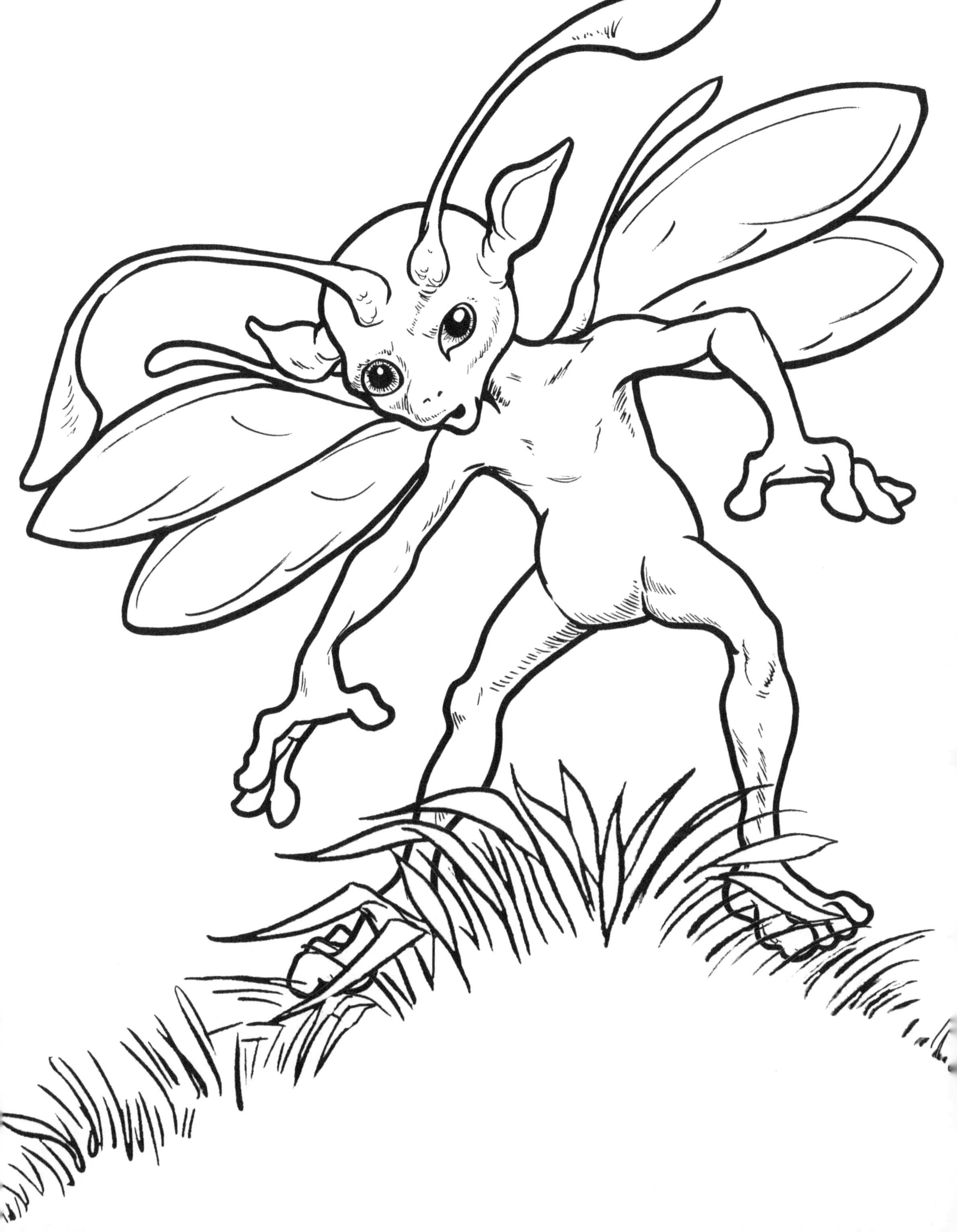

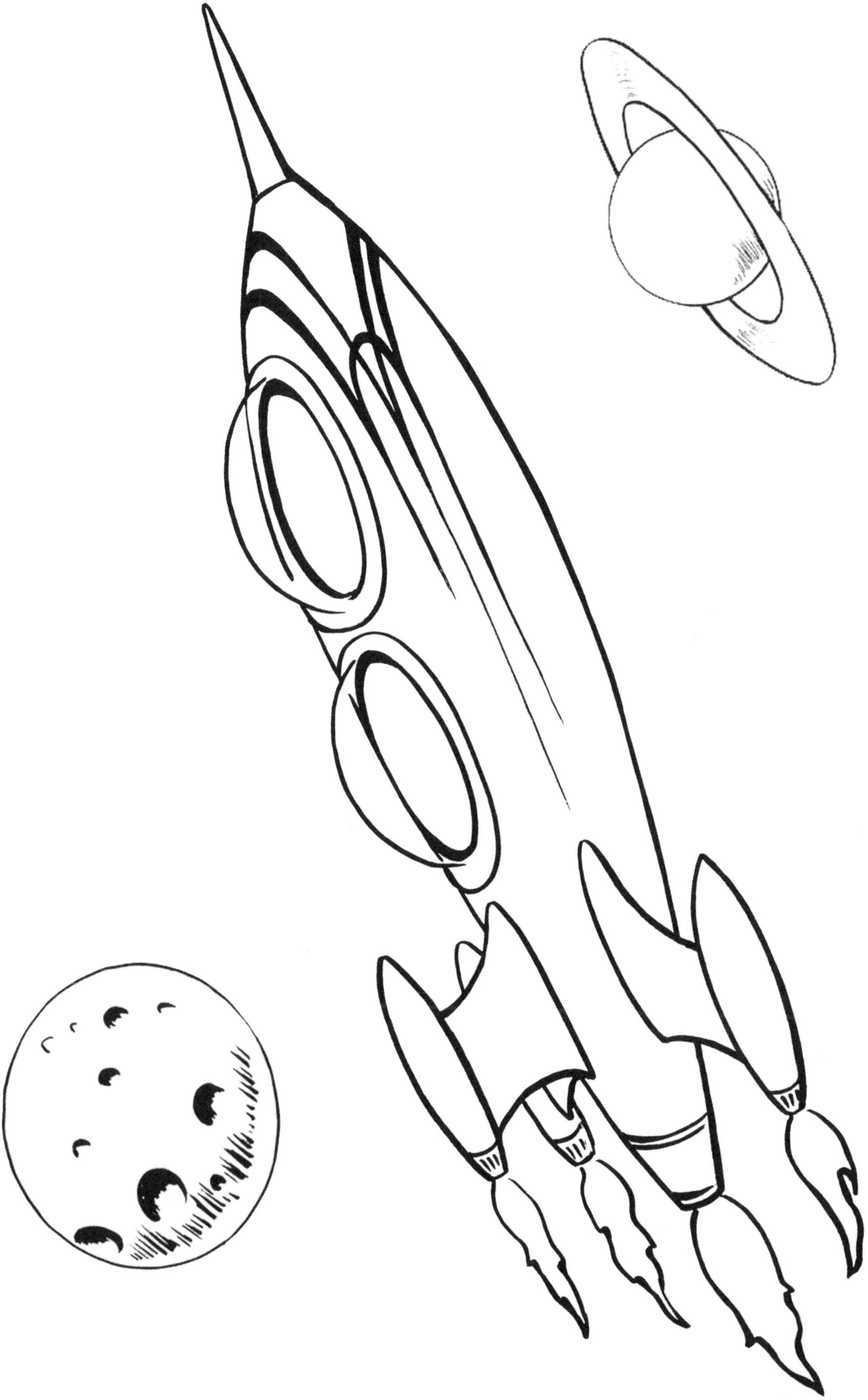

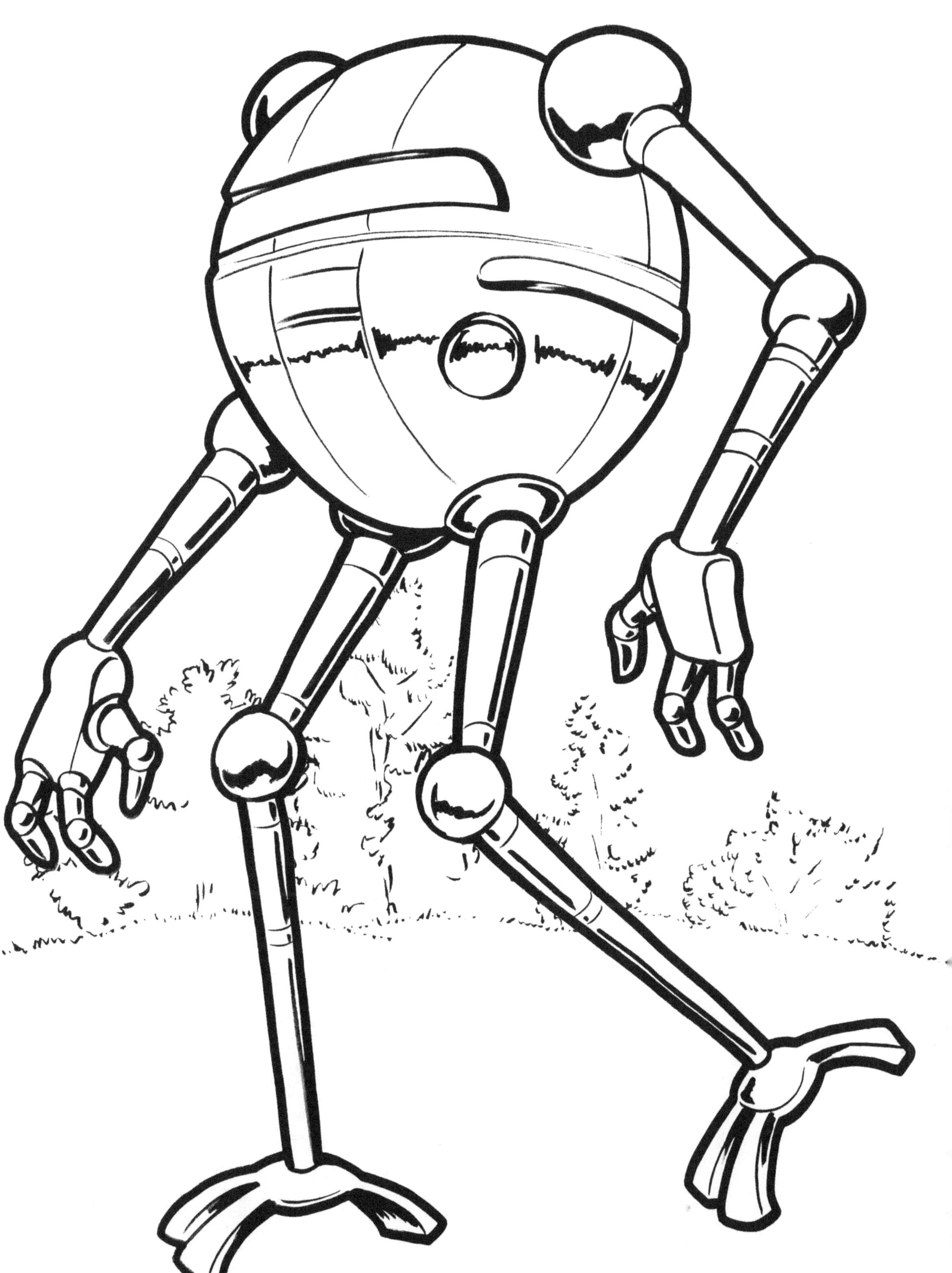

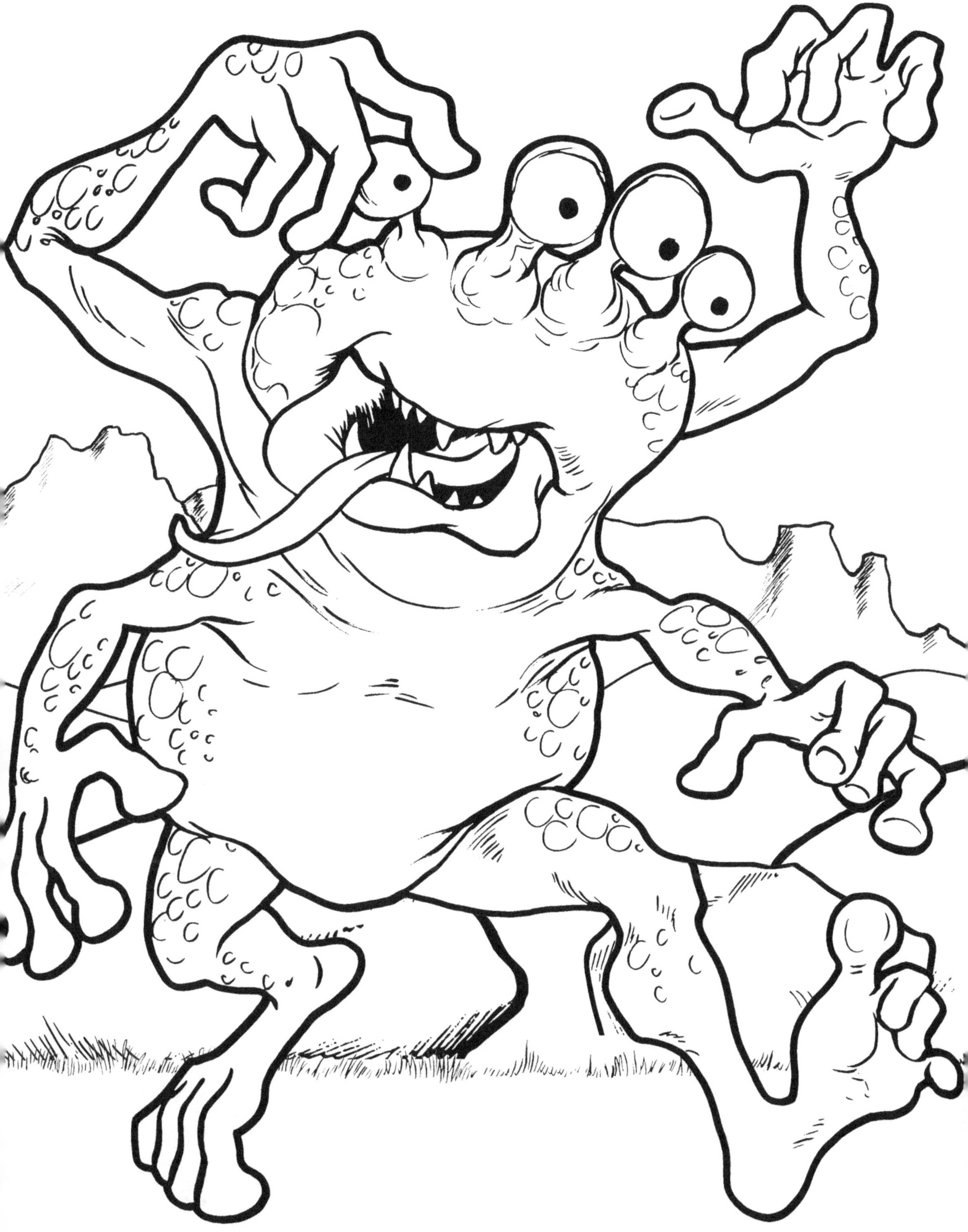

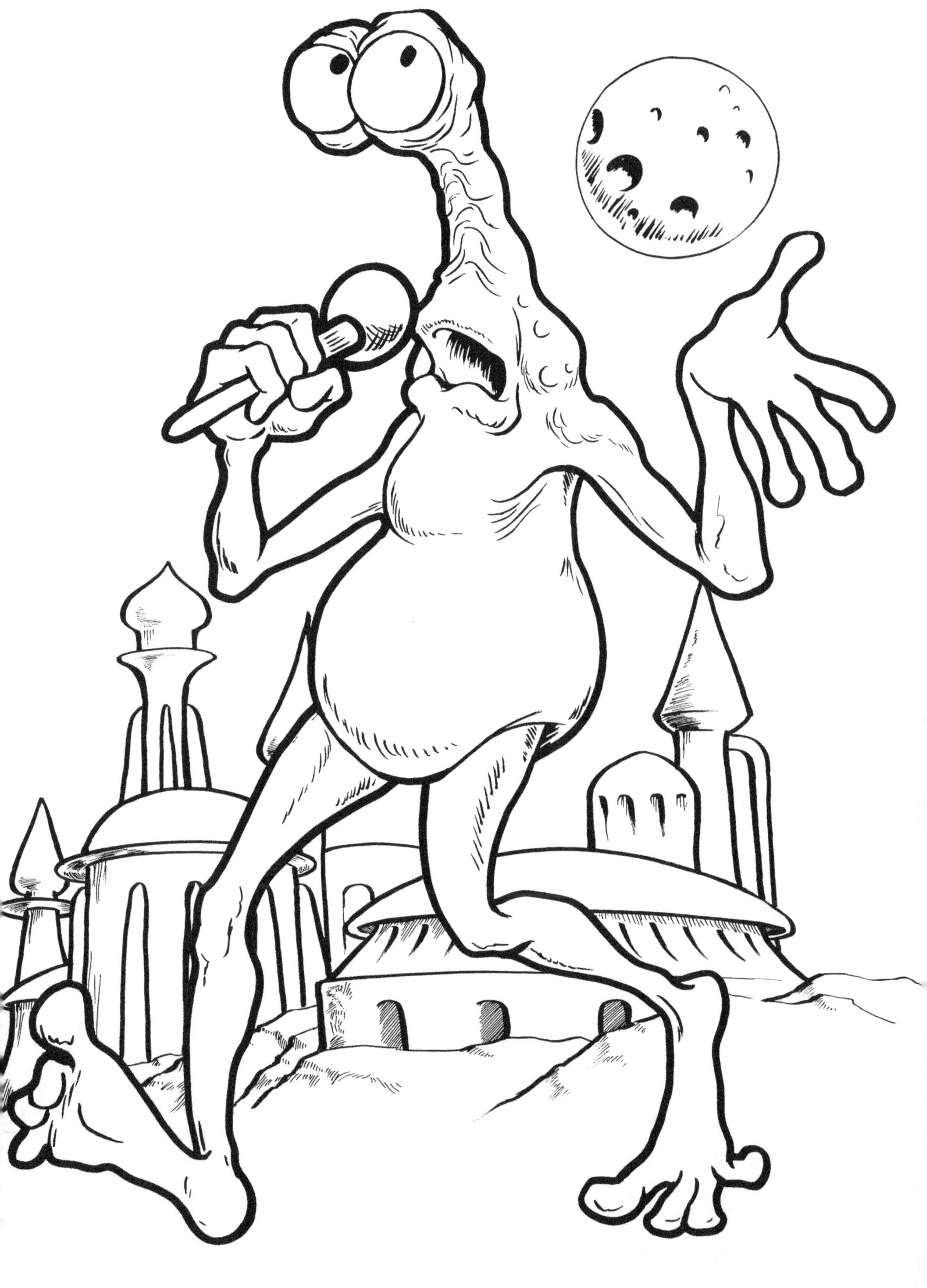

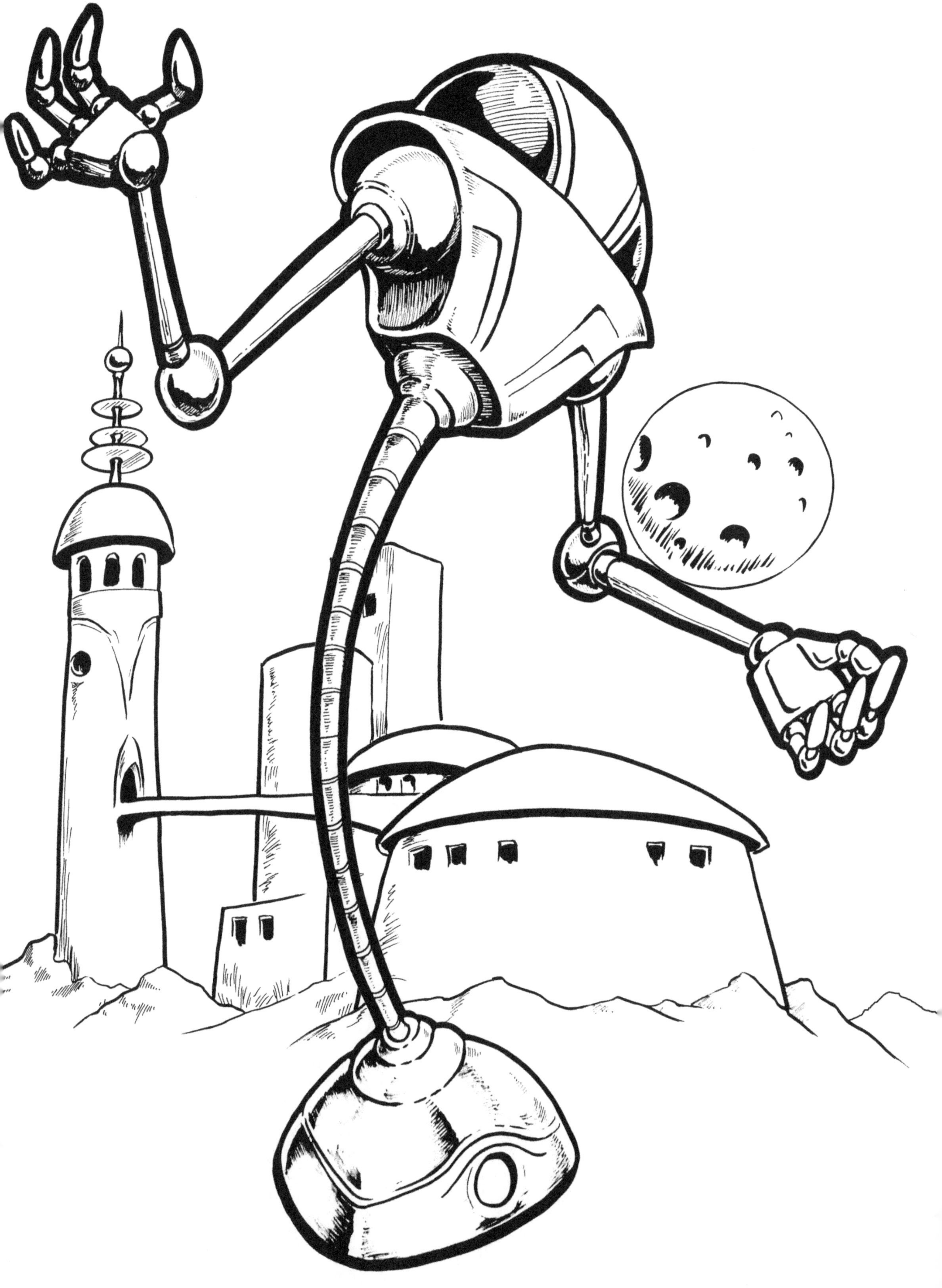

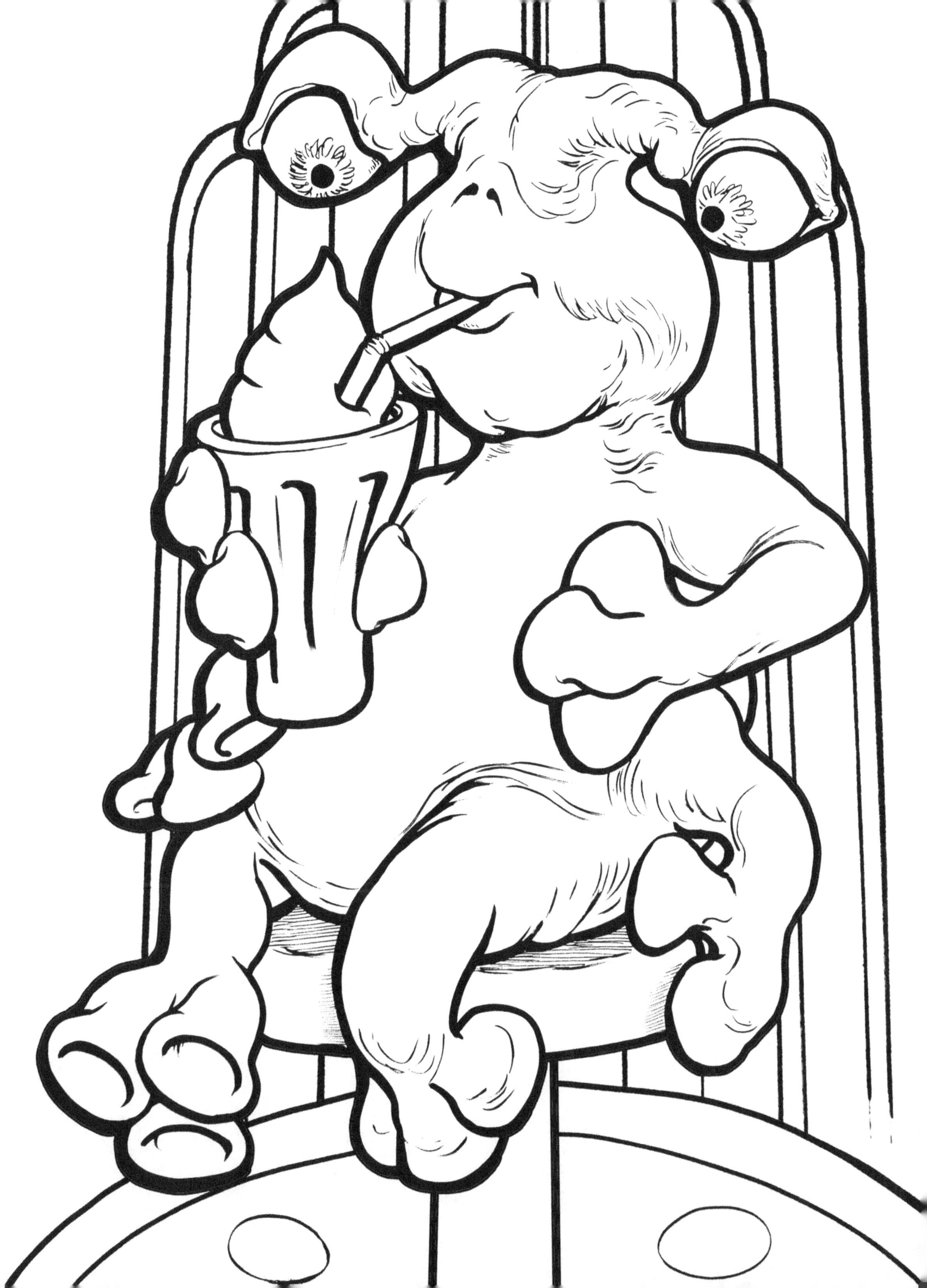

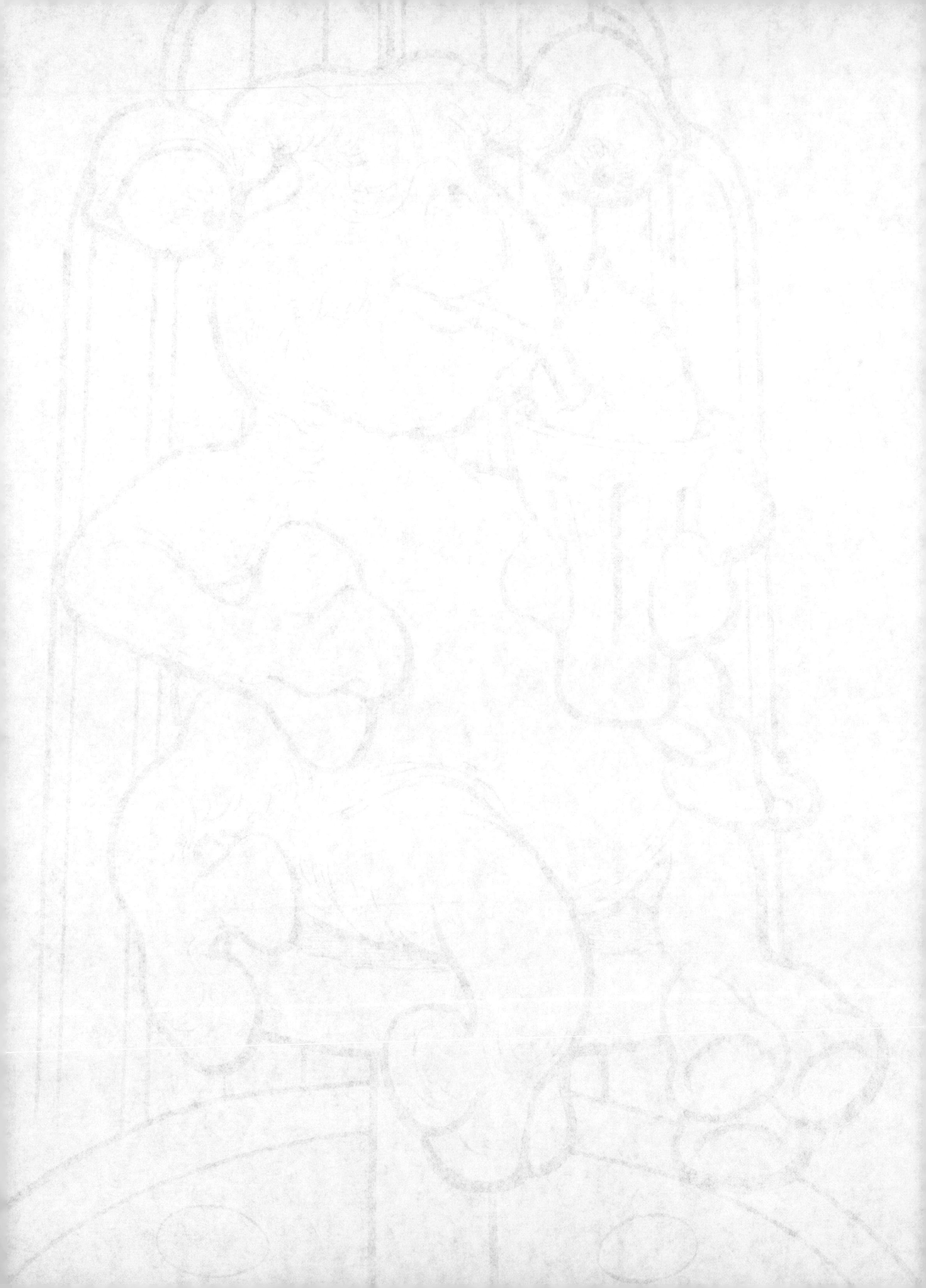

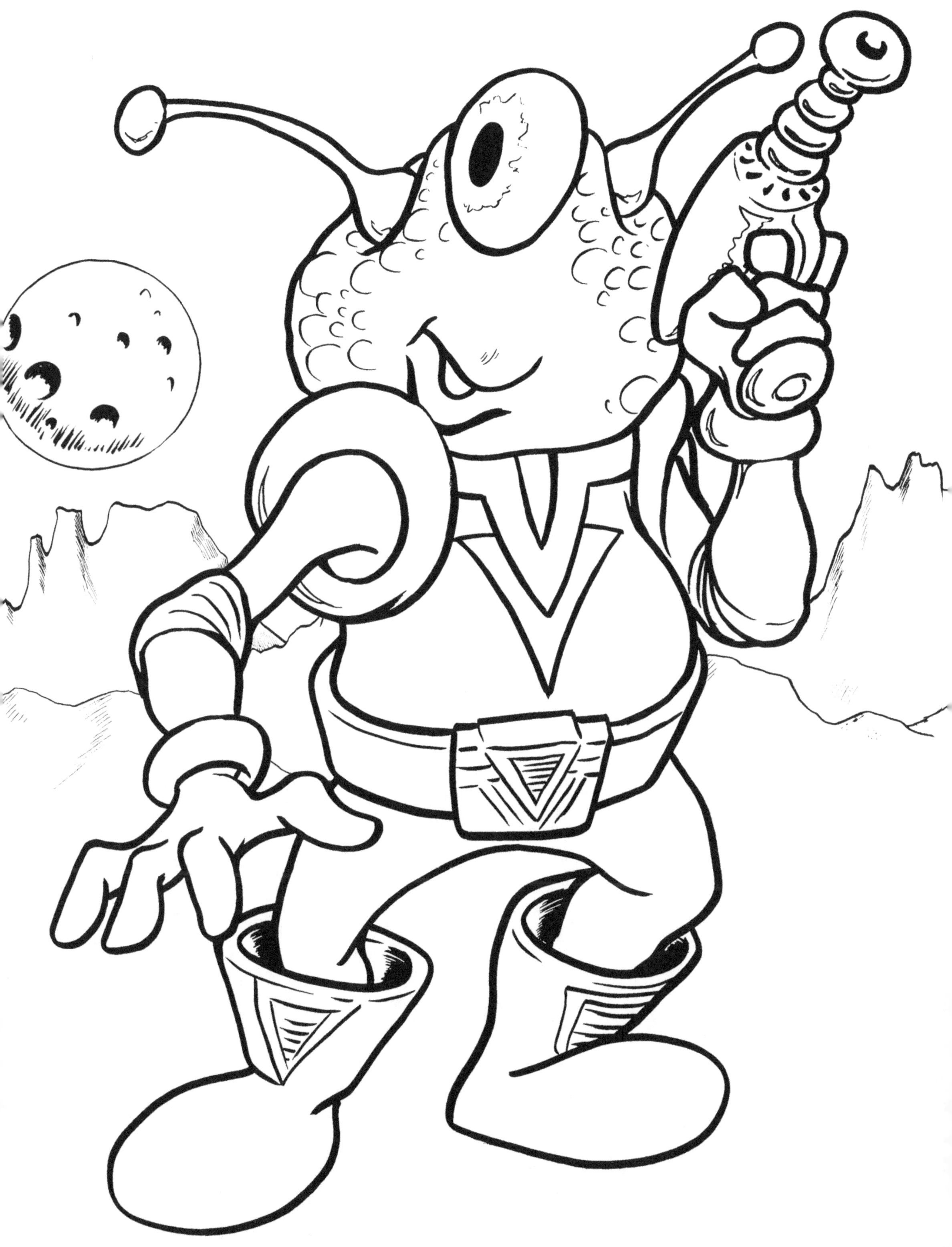

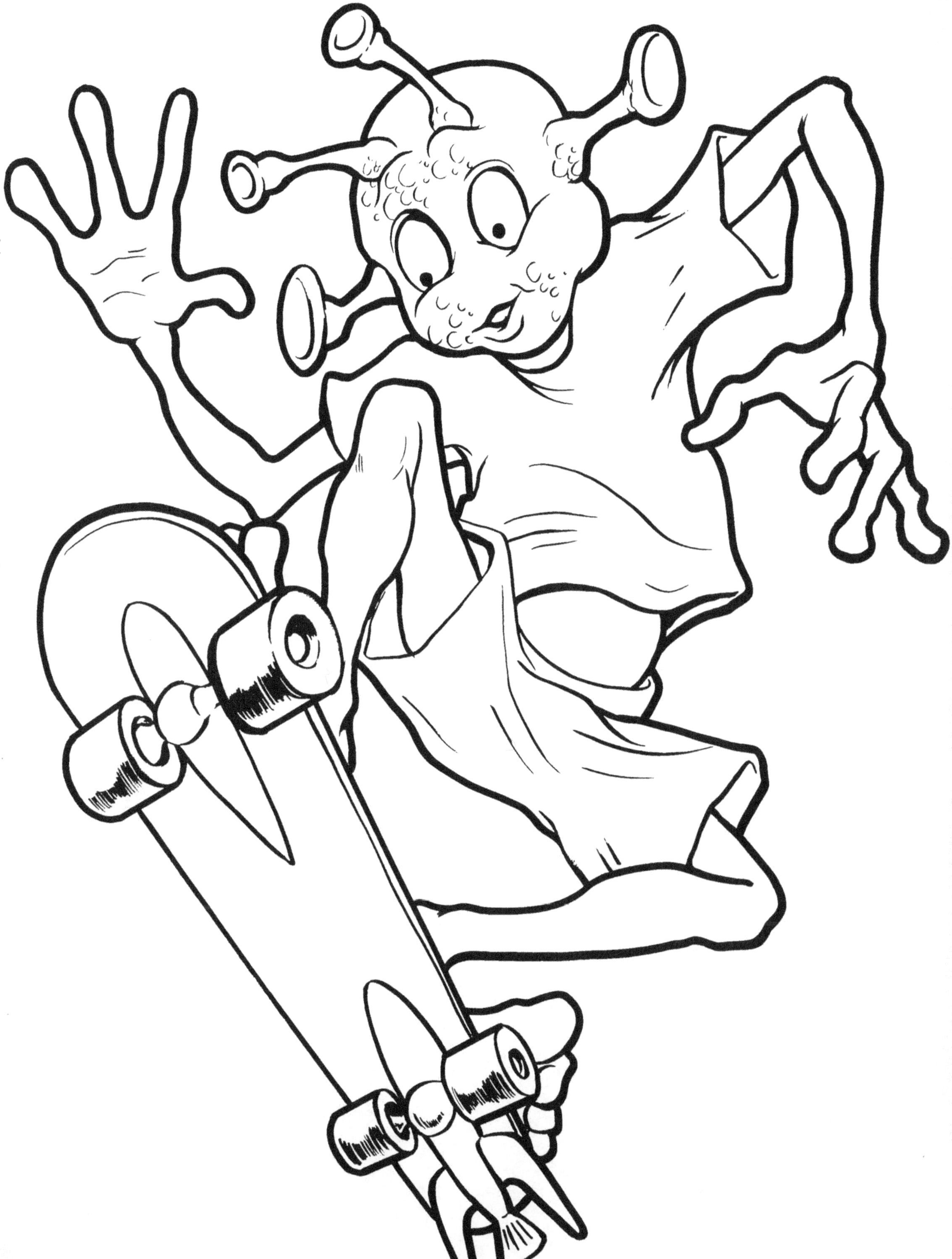

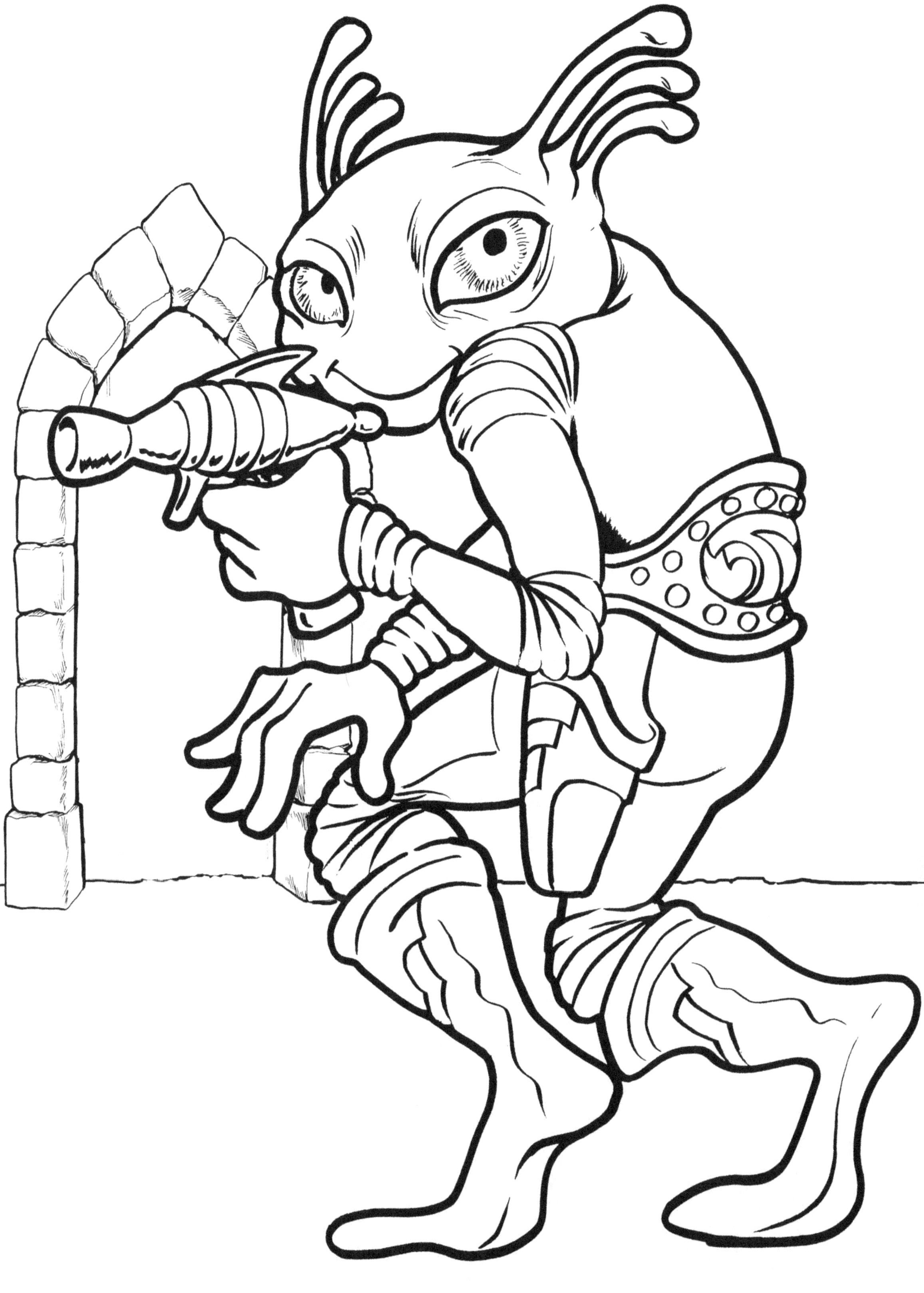

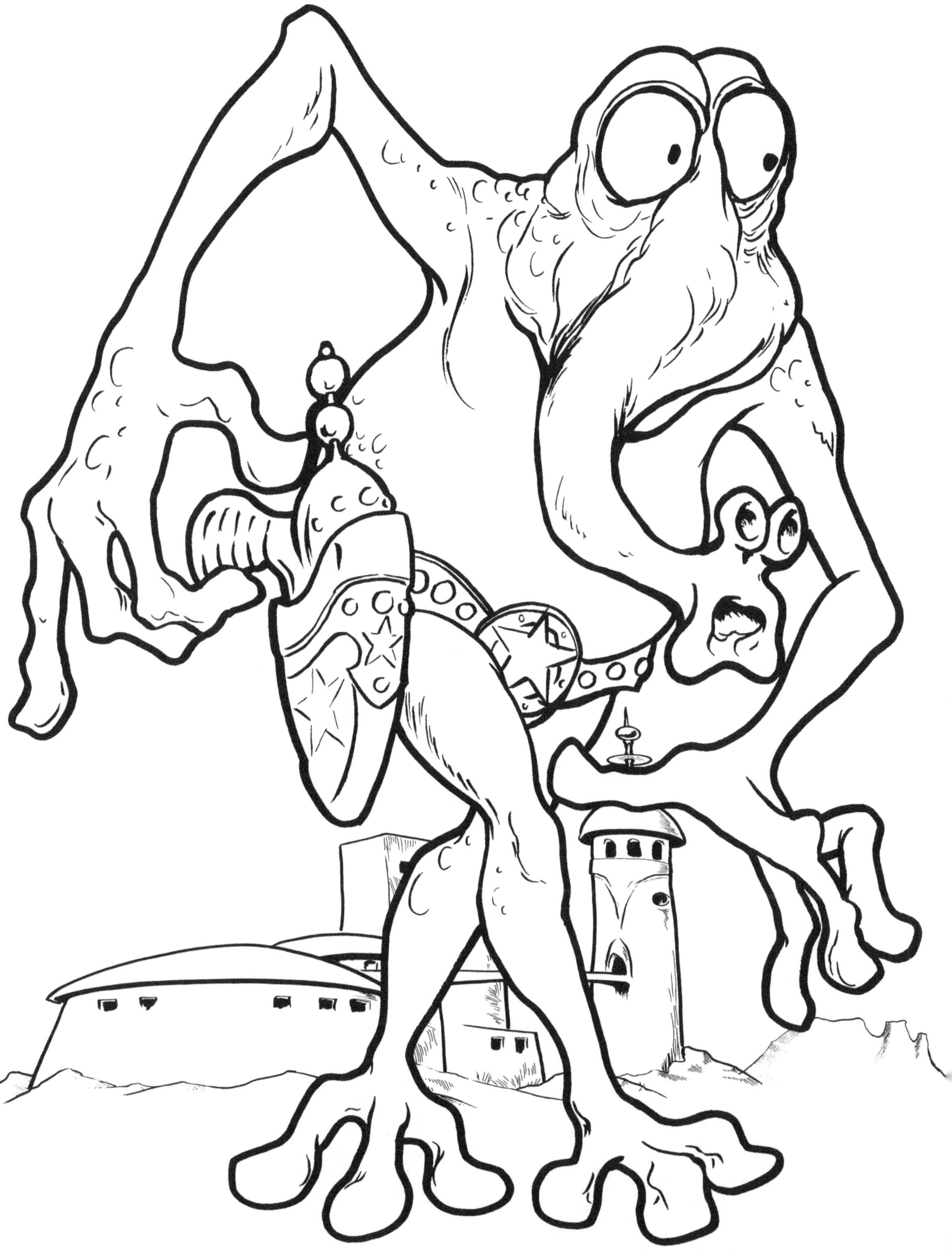

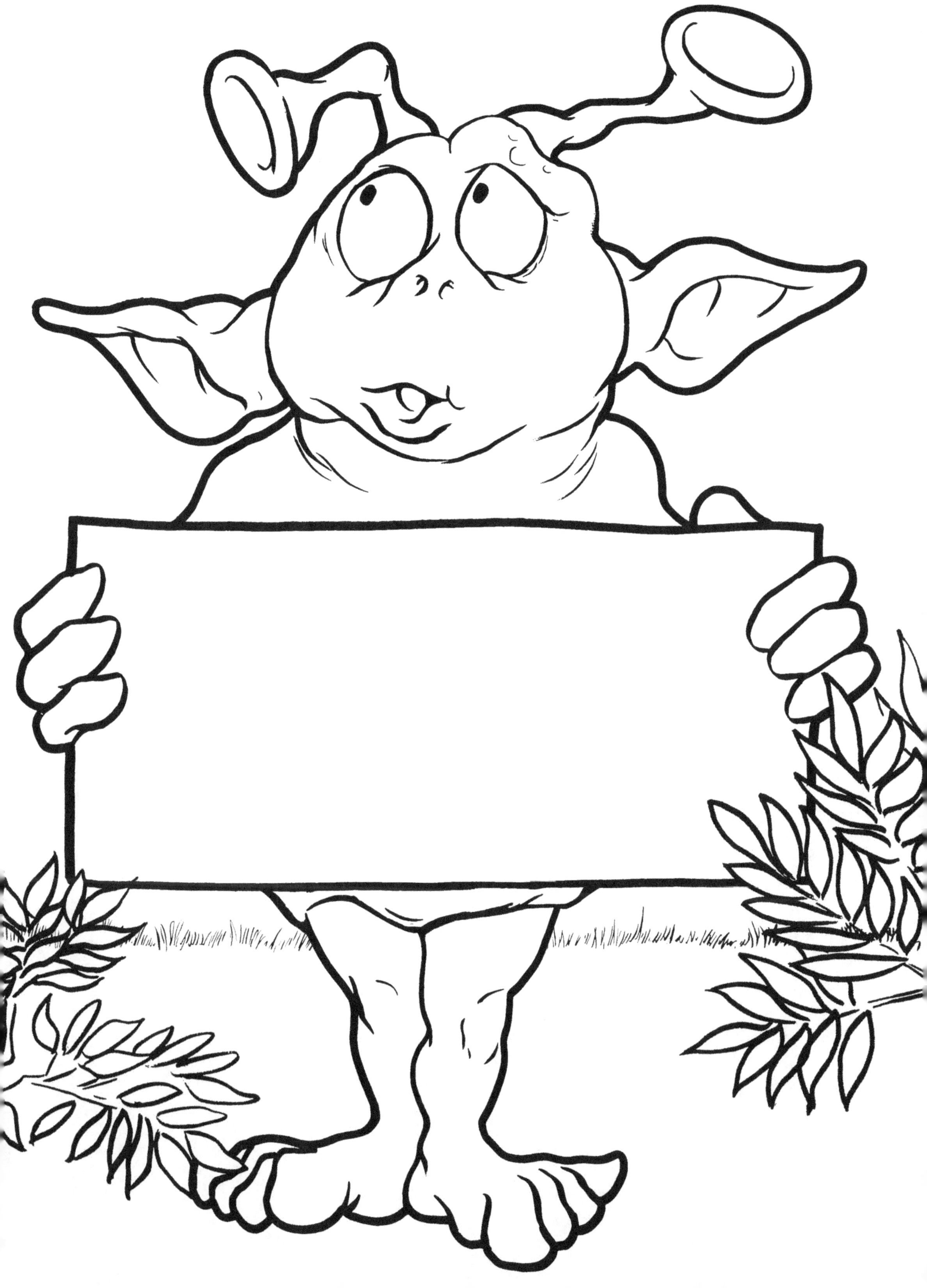

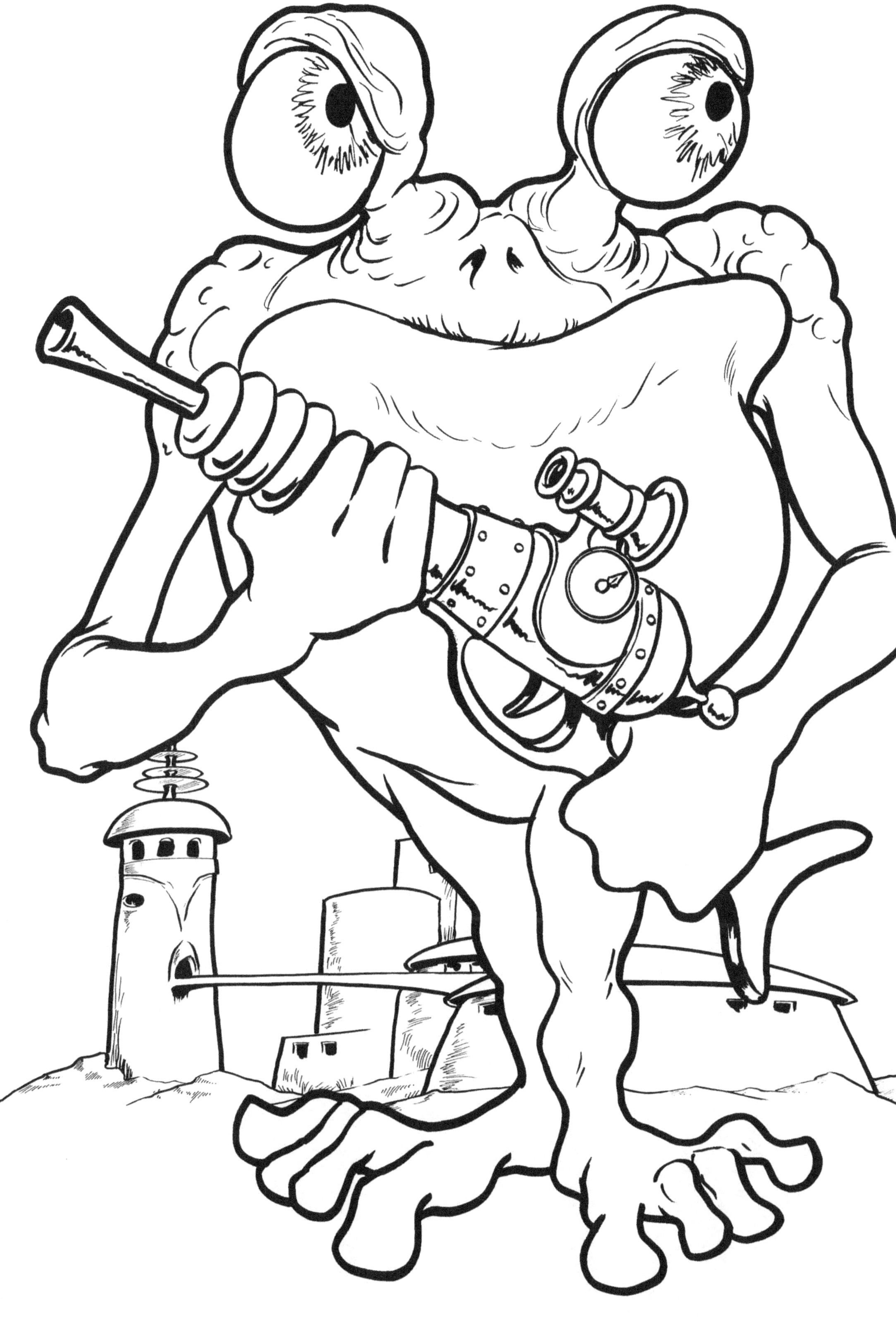

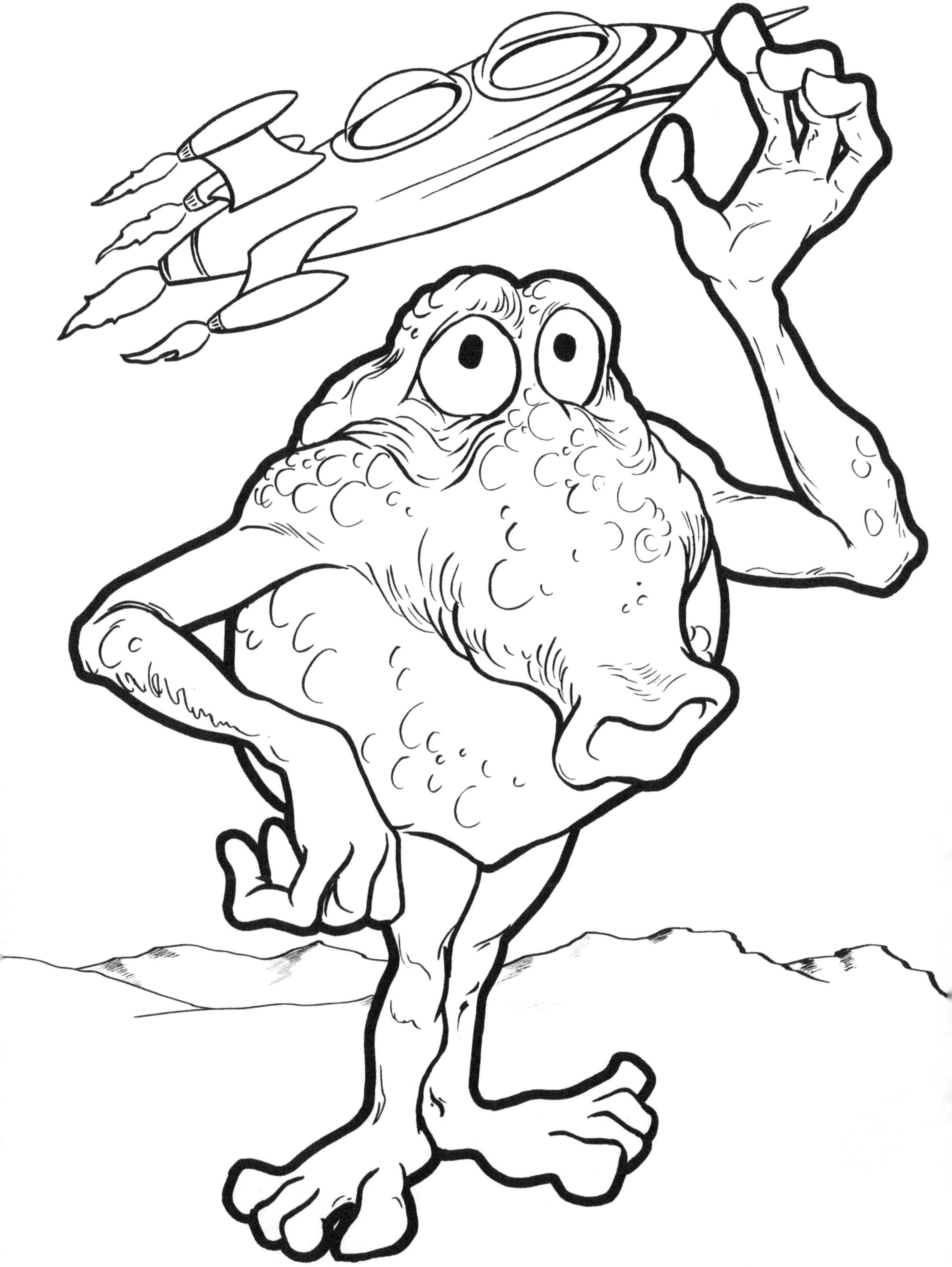

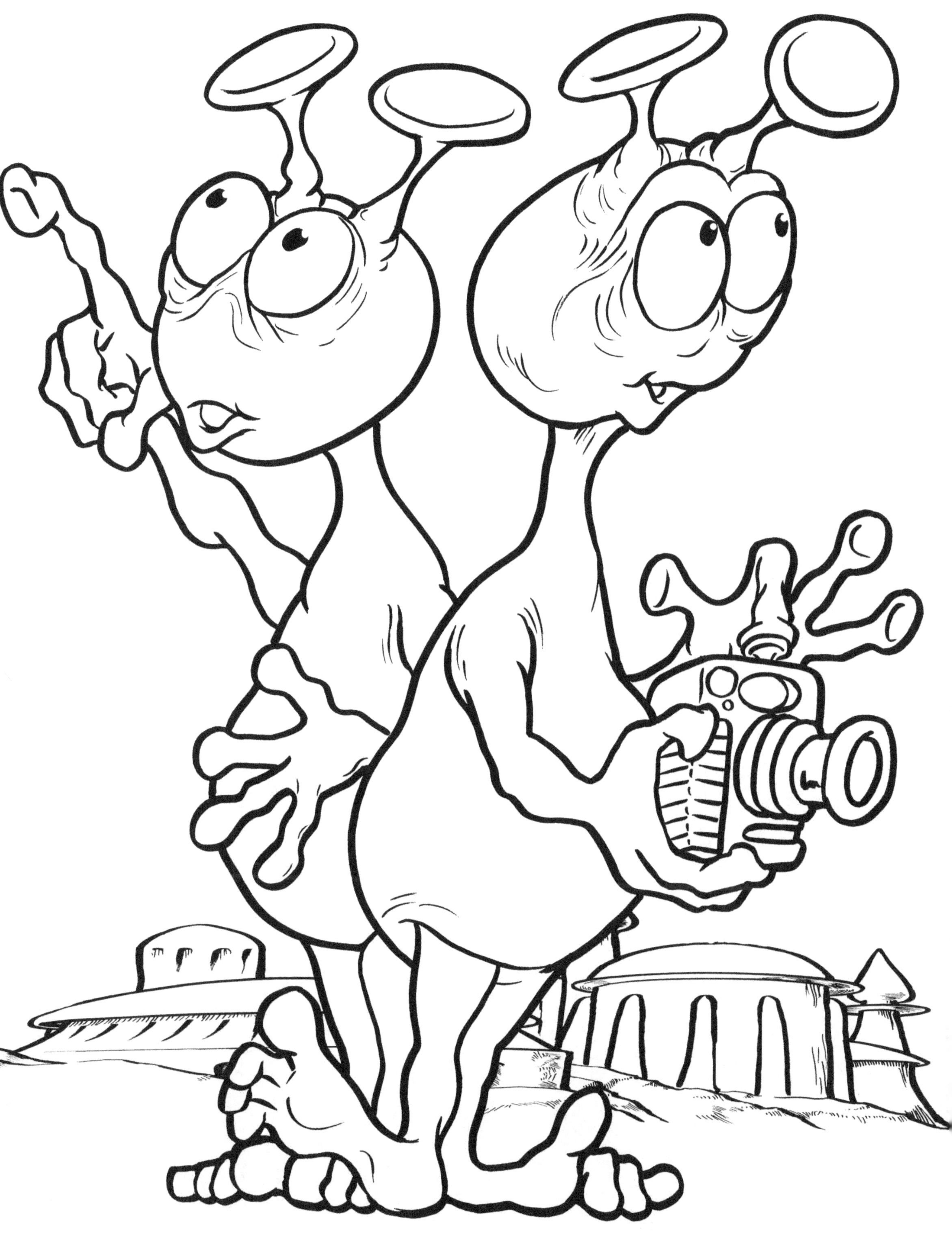

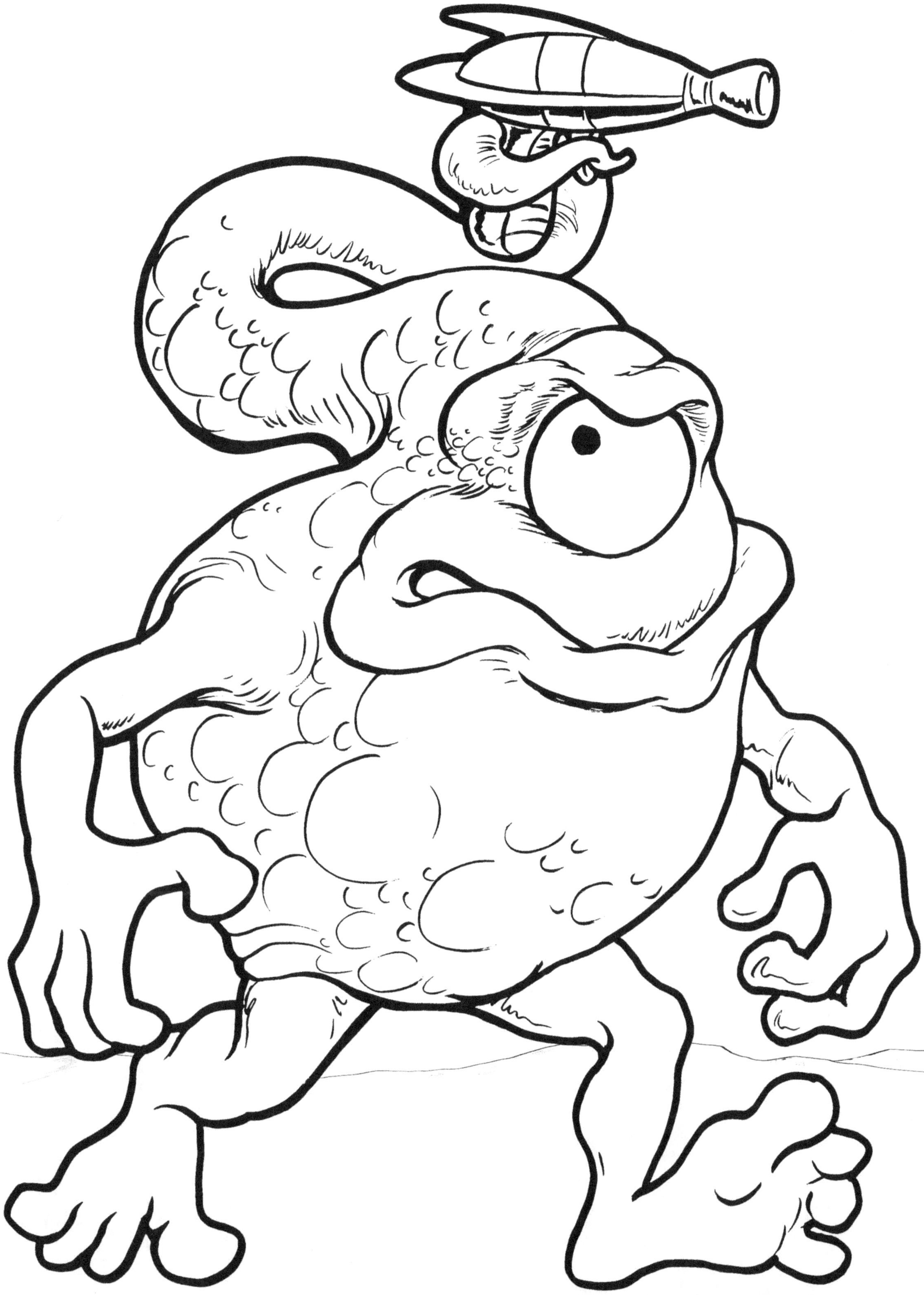

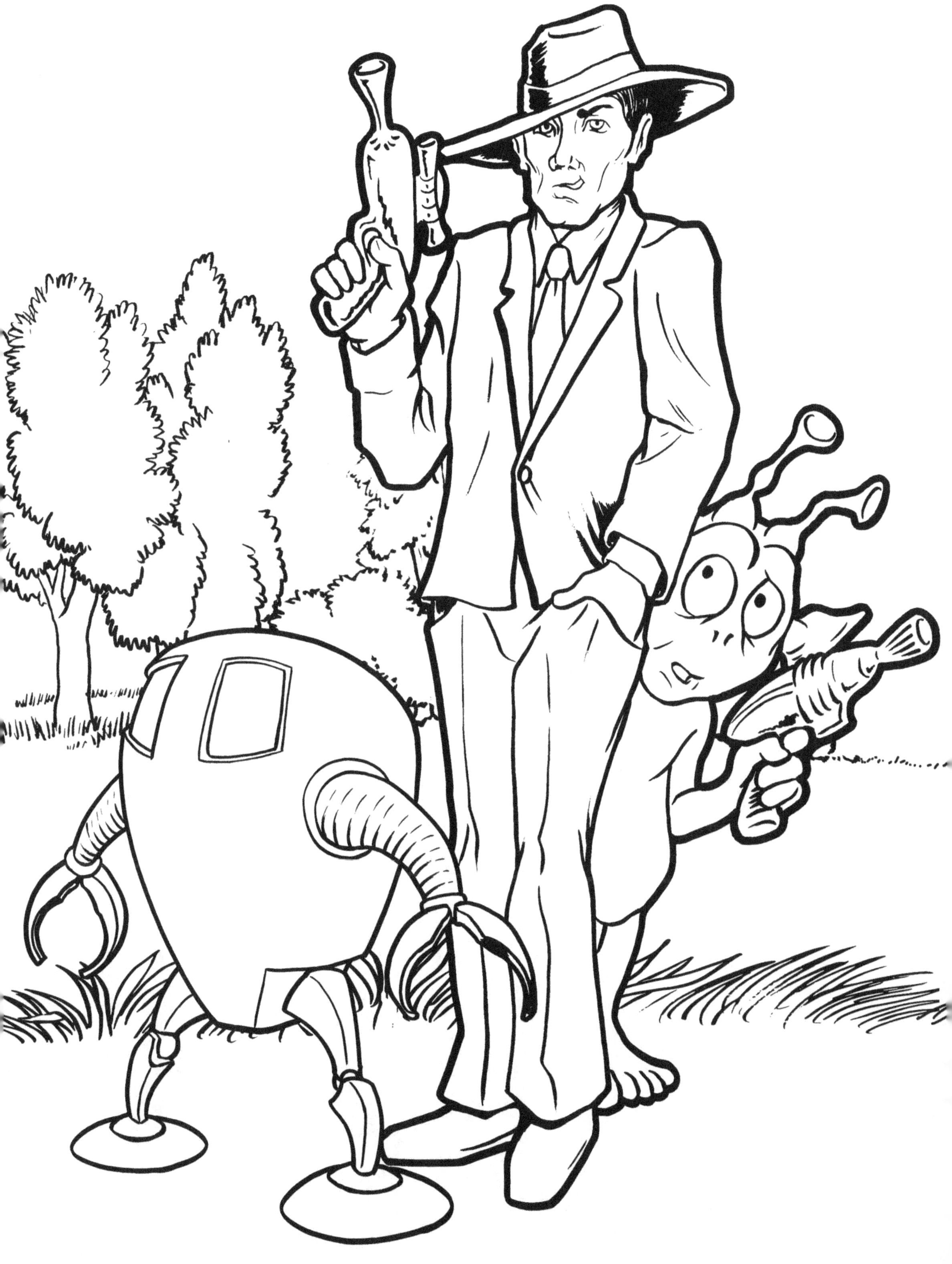

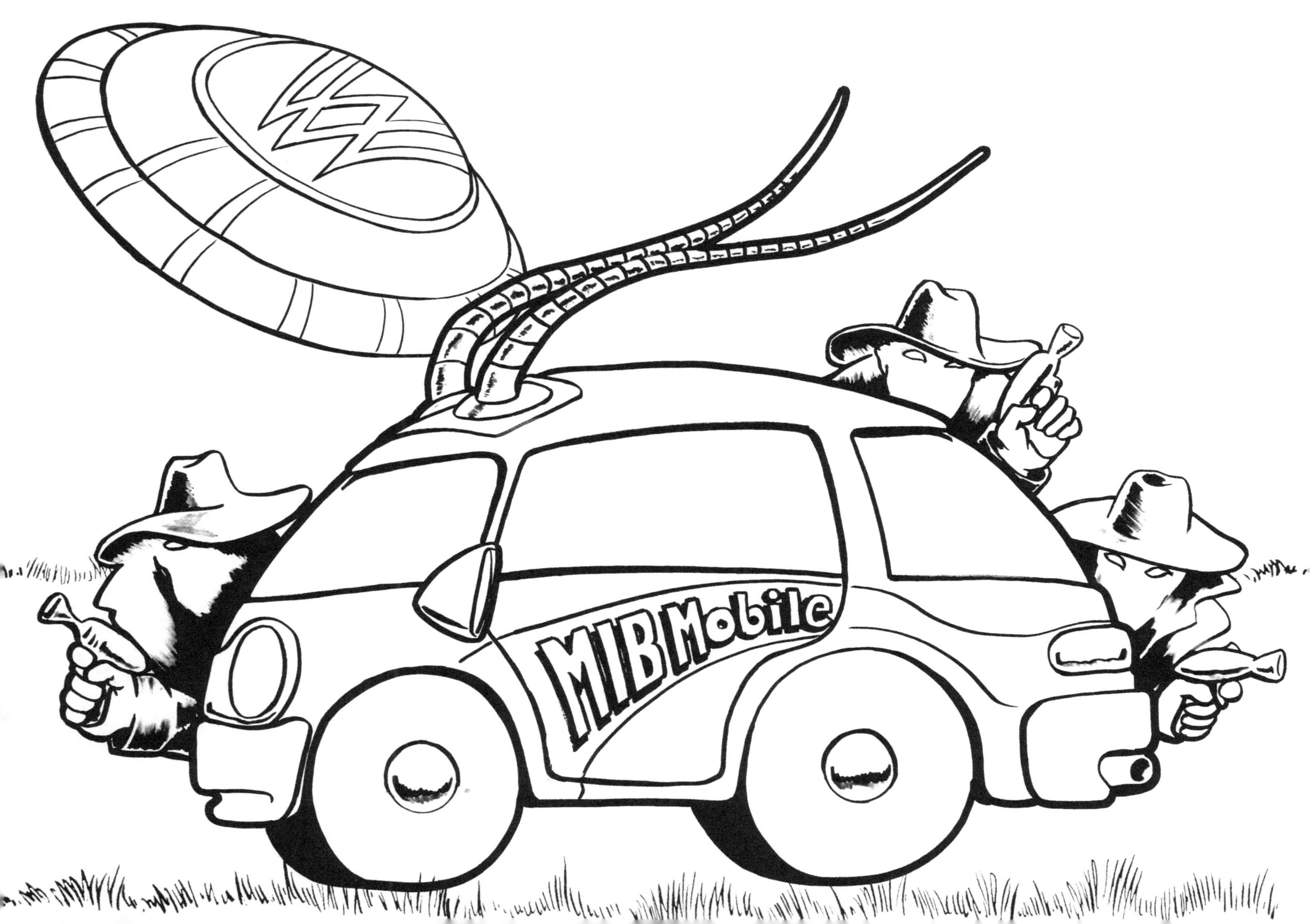
MIB Mobile

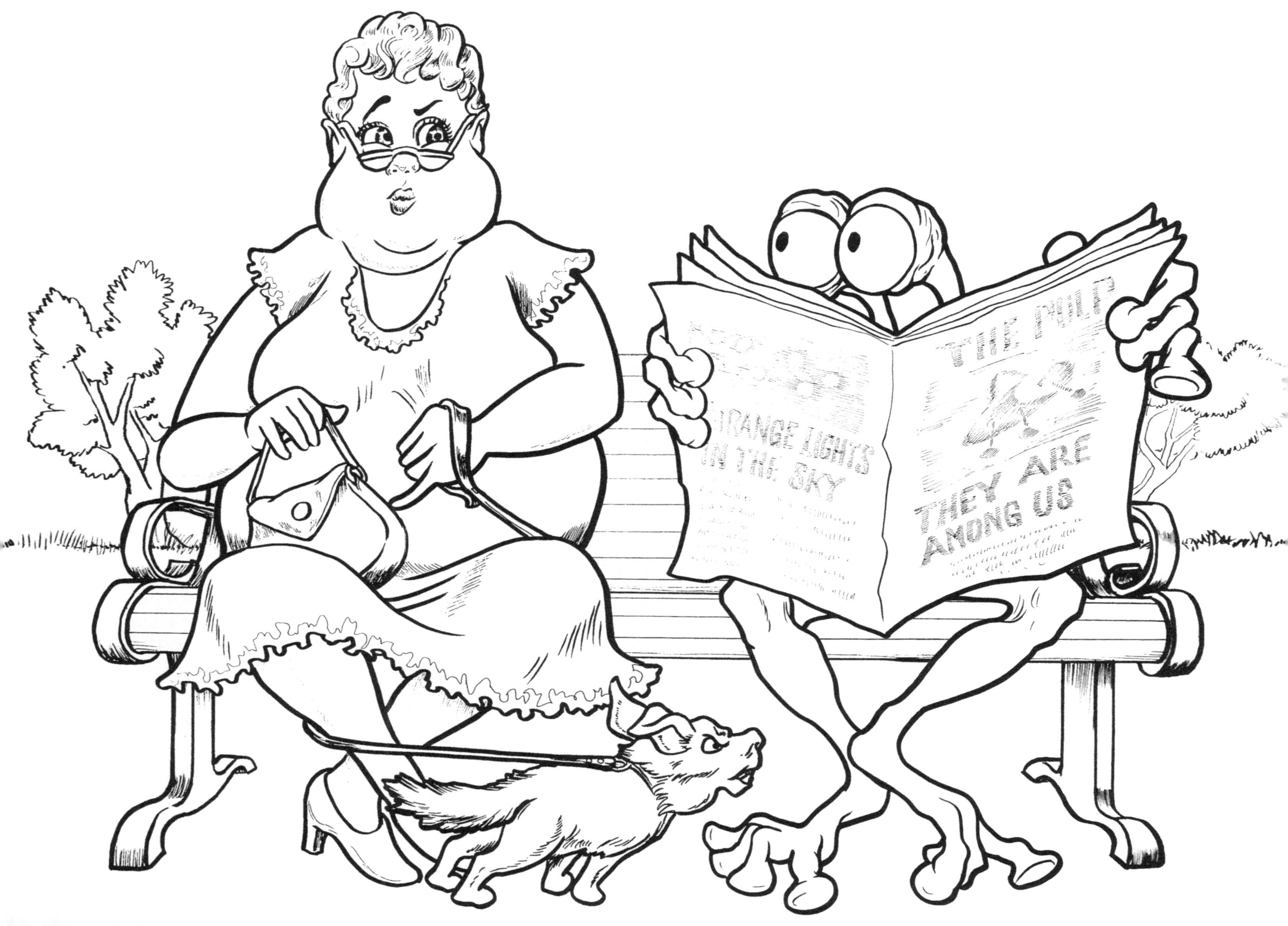
THE PULP
STRANGE LIGHTS IN THE SKY
THEY ARE AMONG US

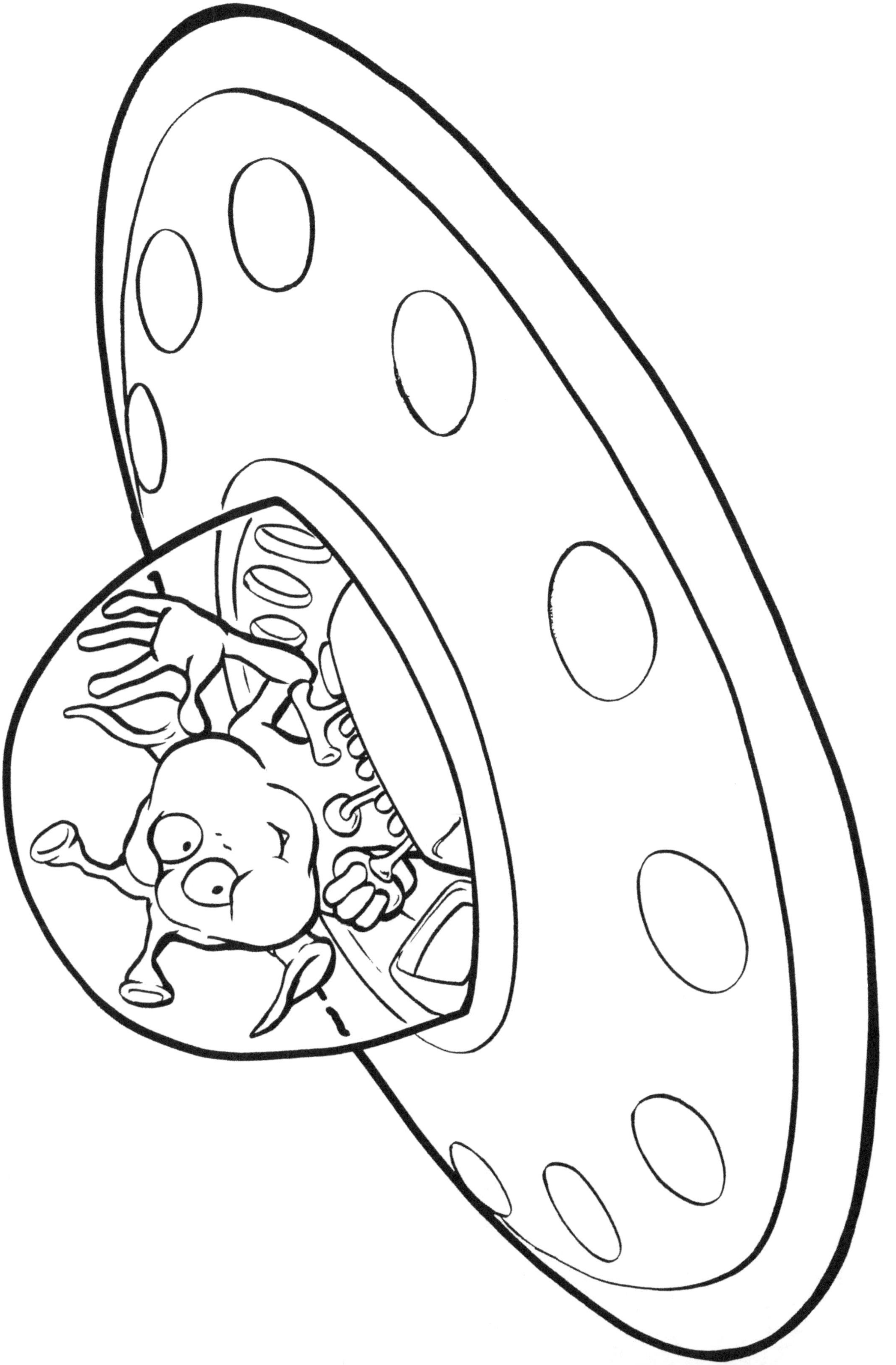

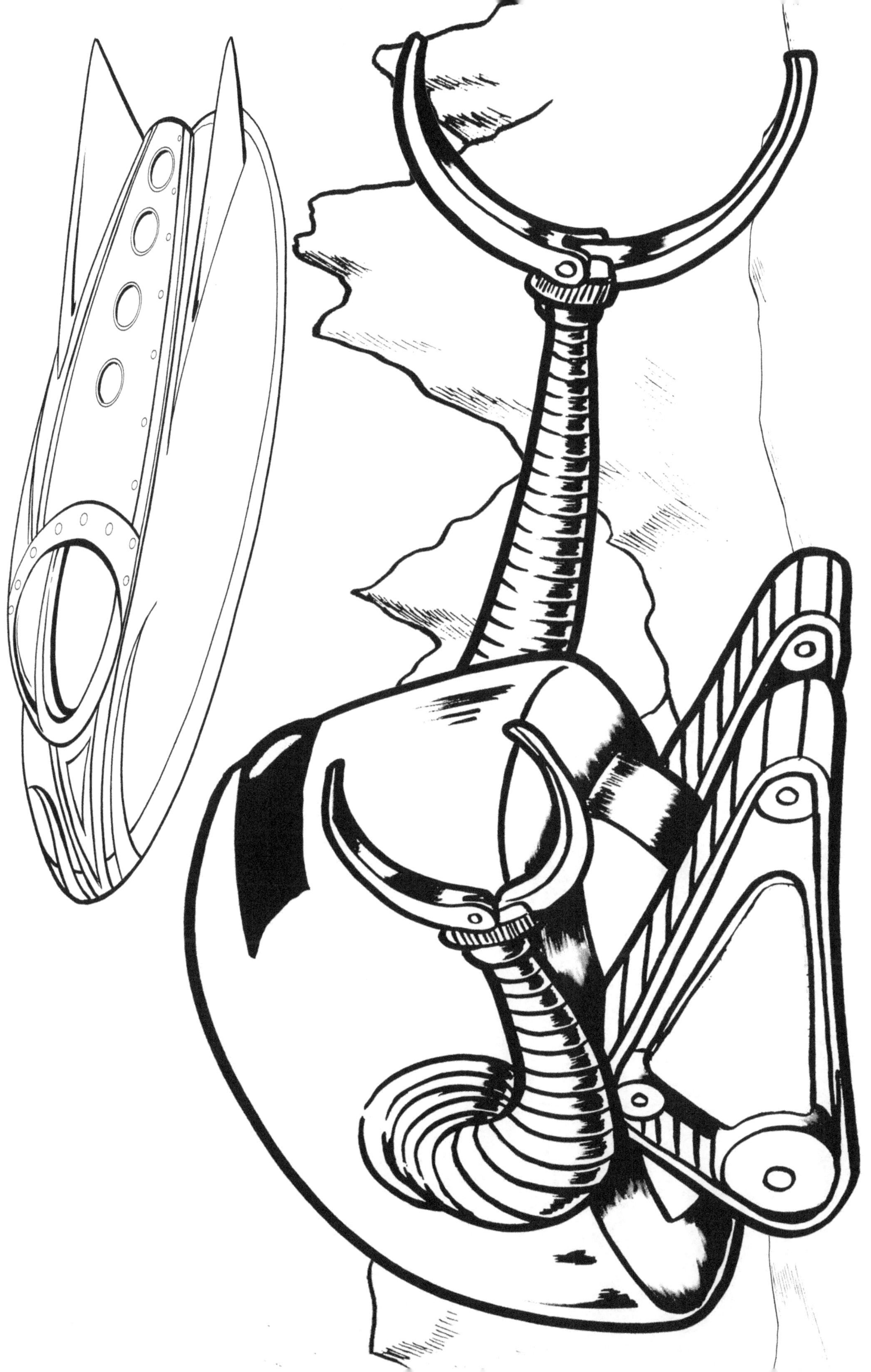

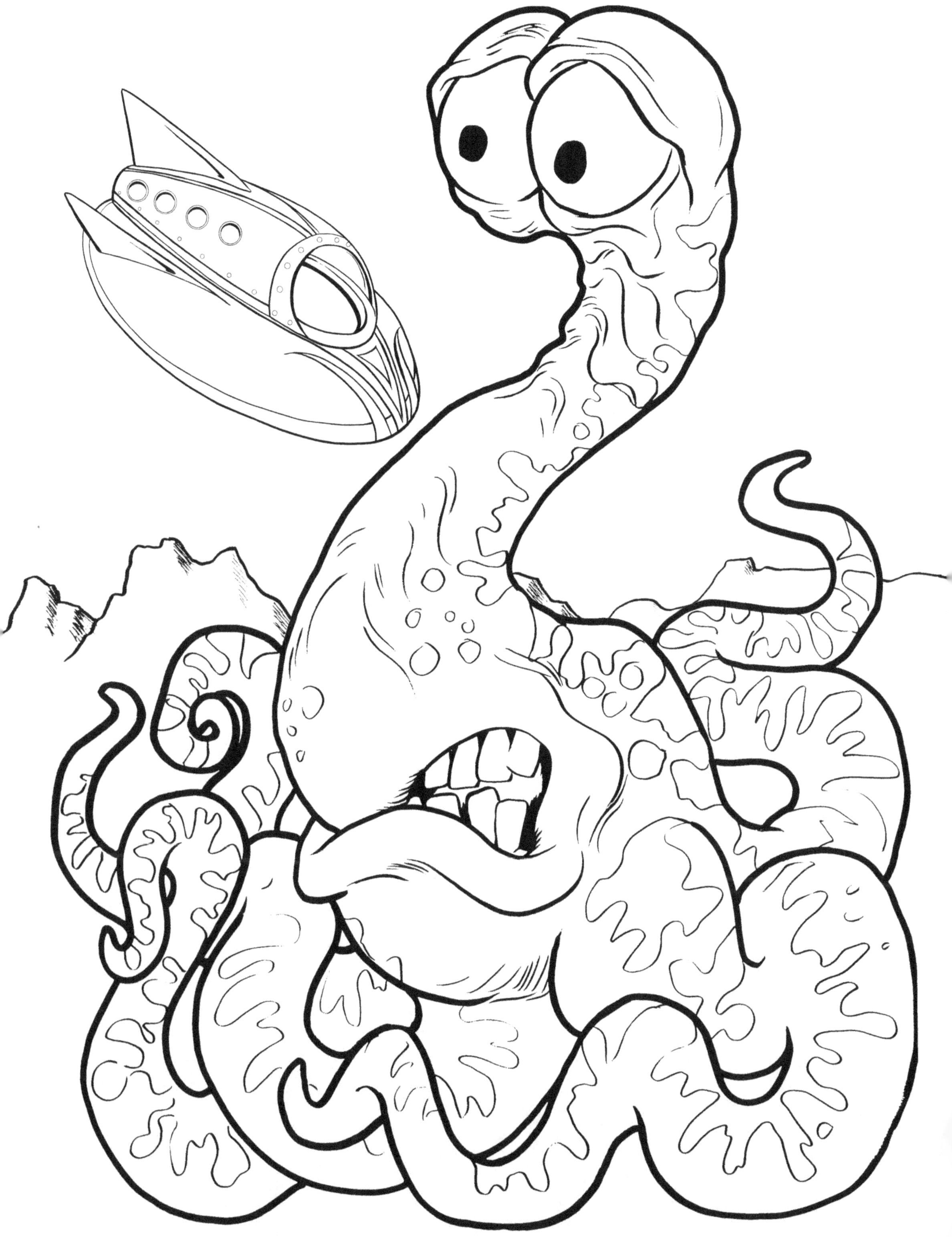

www.ingramcontent.com/pod-product-compliance
Lightning Source LLC
Chambersburg PA
CBHW080611180526
45168CB00007B/2869